From the Camp Kitchen

Meals and Tales Around the Campfire

Dale Fry

Photographs and drawings by

Marty Fry

ISBN 978-1-957077-06-2

Photographs and sketches by Marty Fry

Published by Royal Antler Enterprises LLC

Publishing assistance by BookCrafters, Parker, Colorado.
www.bookcrafters.net

Table of Contents

List of Photographs 1

Introduction 3

He's A Cowboy 9

Canning Mary's Elk Mincemeat 11

Desserts 13

   Elk Mincemeat Pie 14

   Melissa's Pie Crust 14

   Date Nut Bread 15

   Baked Apples with Chocolate Sauce . 16

An Honest Man 21

Sauces 25

   Sourdough Starter 26

   Sourdough Batter 26

   Sausage Gravy 27

   Enchilada Sauce 27

Quick Breads 31

   Sourdough Biscuits 32

   Baking Powder Biscuits 33

   Corn Bread 34

Fall 37

Cow Camp 41

Baked Casseroles 43

   Green Bean Casserole 44

   Mac & Cheese Bake 45

   Veggie Bake 46

   Meat and Vegetable Pot Pie 47

   Chiles Rellenos José 48

Marty's Meat Muffins 49

   Lasagna 50

Bull Run 53

Stovetop Meals 55

   "Bobcat" Stew 56

   Frying Pan Goulash 57

   Fried Tacos 58

   Linda's Calico Beans 59

Rolph the Viking (aka Vicky) 65

Horses and Camping 71

Camp 77

About the Authors 79

List of Photographs

Tree Wolf 2
Skimmer at Lon Hagler SWA 4
In the Blink of an Eye 5
First Meeting 6
Chipmunk in Hiding - Almost 7
Bull on the Rocks 8
Dixie Mare 9
My Mother's Original Mincemeat Recipe 10
Fall Harvesting 13
Chickadee at Home 17
Osprey Fledglings 18
Great Horned Owlet 19
The Elk of Moraine Park 20
The Challenge 21
Night Flight 22
Fiery Sunset 23
Snow and Fire 24
Storm Brewing 25
Hey, It's Cold Out Here 28
Frozen Dinner 29
Pinecones and Frost 30
Spring Storm Colorado Style 31
Jackrabbit Enters Stage Right 34
Heron in Repose 35
Autumn Gold 36
Elk Alert 37
Wilderness FedEx . . . . 38 - 39
Josephine's Cabin 40
Breakfast Feast 41
Laramie River Valley 42

Just Missed 43
Avocet Delight 47
Morning Fog 51
Checking Out the Newbie 52
Winter at Sprague Lake 54
Paintbrush and Pine 55
What do I do now? 57
March of the Trumpeter Swans 58
Winter Hawk 60
As the Clouds Part 61
White-breasted Nuthatch 62
Watching and Waiting 63
Yellow-bellied Marmot 64
Blue Columbine 66
Budding Alfalfa 67
Ghost Image 68
Water Lily Reflection 69
KeSa Mares 70
Monarch Glory 72
Rocky Mountain Parnassian 73
Rawah Pronghorn 74
Sneak Peek 75
Night Camp 76
The End 78

Tree Wolf

2

Introduction

For more than 40 years I have hunted and camped in Colorado's Laramie River Valley. And each year I would meet other hunters who returned to this valley. We would get together for a cup of coffee around the campfire and compare the day's hunting successes or failures. These casual get-togethers eventually became a full-fledged hunting camp where we shared meals and chores and tent space when needed.

Along the way I became the camp cook. Maybe it was because as a young boy, I learned to cook on a wood stove or maybe it was because I liked cooking. Whatever the reason, I looked forward each year to preparing old favorite recipes or trying out new ones. In recent years I have added an oven to my wood stove and have baked pies, birthday cakes, and elk roasts. Many of these recipes are included in the following pages.

For a few years now, my friends keep telling me that I should write a book with some of their favorite recipes and maybe add some of the stories I told them about growing up on a ranch outside Estes Park. I finally listened and this is the result.

To make the book more than just another campfire cookbook, I asked my beautiful wife, Marty, if I could use her nature and wildlife photographs and sketches to illustrate the book. She agreed.

You won't find exotic ingredients or gourmet recipes in this book, just simple, hearty meals for hungry hunters or hikers returning from a long day out in the forest. And while the emphasis of this book is on meals for camping, all the recipes can be prepared at home for your own hungry hunters returning from a long day out in the urban jungle.

It is my hope that this book will be a treat, not only to your palate but also to your eye and your spirit. So don't wait! Start cooking and enjoy.

Remember, the coffee pot's always on.

Dale Fry

Skimmer at Lon Hagler SWA

In the Blink of an Eye

First Meeting

Chipmunk in Hiding ... Almost

Bull on the Rocks

He's A Cowboy

No…
His spurs don't hit the point of the shoulder first jump out.
His horse don't slide to a stop when he ropes a calf.
He don't tie in 7 flat.
He don't bulldog or ride bulls.

This cowboy ranches
In a beat up felt hat, patched jeans, and high-heeled boots scuffed and worn.

Come Winter he's feeding hay each day with a team and sled.
In Spring he's up all hours in all weather, pulling calves.
And Summer means fixing fence, irrigating, riding, and doctoring.
Then it's haying season.
With Fall he's gathering and shipping.

Come Winter and it starts all over.
It's a way of life he wouldn't trade.

He's a cowboy

Dixie Mare

Elk or Venison Mincemeat

6 lbs. (neck or Brisket) covered, in water, cook till tender, about 3 hours. Cool, Put through coarse blade of food chopper with 3 lbs. suet (white Kidney beef suet) and 8 pounds tart red apples, pared, cored + cubed.

In large kettle, blend with 12 cups sugar, 10 cups dried Currants, 15 cups raisins, 10 teaspoons grated orange peel, 6 tsp. grated lemon peel, 12 cups water, 3 cups apple Cider, 6 tsp salt, 3 tsp ground (drained) nutmeg, 1 can sour pitted cherries. 3 cups chopped walnuts.

Cover, simmer 1-2 hours —

Can in 1 qt. wide mouth jars.

When ready to use for pies (over)

cut up another apple, add about ½ cup cider.

If you want to - buy a small bottle of imitation rum flavoring and add 1 tablespoon to mixture

Bake in 2 crust pie tin at 400° for 35 to 45 min.

My mother's original mincemeat recipe. Written around 1951.

Canning Mary's Elk Mincemeat

This recipe is a variation of a recipe my mother, Mary Fry, used for over 50 years. The only real difference is that Mary used the neck or brisket and cooked it for 3 hours before grinding it then adding the rest of the ingredients. I have shortened the process, but not the taste, by using ground elk meat that does not have added fat or suet.

Canning instructions are included for those of you, like us, who don't have a clue where to start. The mincemeat can be used for pies after about 3 months but the longer you wait, the better it gets.

What You Need   Makes 18 quarts

6 lbs. ground elk meat – no added fat or suet
3 lbs. beef suet
11 cups water
12 cups sugar
6 tsp salt
3 cups apple cider
10 cups currents, dried
15 cups raisins
2 cans pie cherries in juice (not in filling)
3 tsp nutmeg, ground
1 Tbsp pure rum extract (optional)
10 tsp orange peel, grated
6 tsp lemon peel, grated
8 lbs. apples, tart cooking apples are best

Putting It Together

Combine all ingredients except the orange peel, lemon peel and apples into a large pot or kettle. Cook on medium heat for 1 hour, stirring occasionally.

Meantime, core and peel apples, cut into small pieces. Grate orange and lemon peel. Add orange peel, lemon peel, and apples and cook for 1 additional hour. Turn heat to low and simmer while preparing and filling canning jars.

Canning

Recommended equipment:
    Large canning pot (should come with canning rack to hold 6 jars)
    Canning funnel, tongs, jar lifter
    18 Ball 1-quart mason wide-mouth canning jars with bands and lids
    Optional: bottle wrench, and magnetic lid lifter

Preparation:
    Wash jars, lids, and bands in hot water. Fill the canning pot to jar height with water and bring to a boil.

Packing and processing jars:
    Fill jars with mincemeat to within ½ inch of the top. Make sure rim of jar is clean and dry, then put on lid and tighten ring. Put jars in boiling water and add hot water until the jars are covered by ~1 inch of water. Leave about 2 inches between each jar. The jars must not touch each other.

    Boil the jars for 40-45 minutes, adding water to keep the jars covered if necessary. Remove jars with tongs or jar lifter and place on wood or cloth surface, making sure jars are not touching. Let jars cool for 12 hours and then store for at least 3 months.

Testing seals:
    After jars are cooled, test seal by pressing on the center of the lid. If there is any movement, the lid did not seal. The mincemeat must be reprocessed or used immediately.

Note:
    You can sometimes hear a lid pop as the jars are cooling. This means the jars are sealed.

Desserts

Fall Harvesting

Elk Mincemeat Pie

See Canning Mary's Elk Mincemeat for instructions on preparing the filling.

What You Need

1 quart mincemeat
¼ cup cinnamon apple sauce
1 tsp rum extract
1 nine-inch double pie crust. See Melissa's Pie Crust Recipe

Putting It Together

Line 9-inch pie plate with pie crust. Mix ingredients together and spoon into pie plate. Cover with second pie crust, crimp edges and cut 3-4 vent holes in the top.

Bake at 425° for 45 minutes or until top crust is golden brown.

Melissa's Pie Crust

I could never make a good pie crust, so I asked my friend Melissa for her recipe. And I'm thankful I did. This recipe makes 2 crusts.

What You Need

2 cups flour
¾ tsp salt
⅔ cup butter/shortening
¼ cup cold (iced) water
½ tsp white vinegar

Putting It Together

Mix flour and salt. Cut in butter or shortening with pastry cutter until it is pea size. Stir in water and vinegar until dough holds together when shaped into a ball. Roll out on floured surface until you get the desired size and thickness.

Date Nut Bread

The original recipe came from Reader's Digest. But I experimented with it and here is what I came up with.

What You Need

½ cup white sugar
½ cup brown sugar
1 tsp baking soda
1 tsp salt
1 cup water
4 Tbsp (½ stick) melted butter
1 tsp rum extract
1½ cups flour (add 3 Tbsp if at high altitude)
1 cup pitted, chopped fresh dates (not candied)
½ cup chopped walnuts

Putting It Together

Mix white and brown sugar, baking soda, and salt together in a large bowl. Add water, butter, rum and stir until sugar is dissolved. Add flour and hand beat 1 minute (~ 100 strokes). Add dates and nuts and mix well. Mixture should be more of a batter than a stiff dough.

Pour into greased bread loaf pan.

Bake at 375° for 45 minutes. Check the center of the loaf with a toothpick. When it comes out clean, the bread is done.

Baked Apples with Chocolate Sauce

You can adjust this recipe depending on how much sauce you want to cover the number of apples you bake.

What You Need

8-10 apples
2 large bars dark chocolate
¼ cup cream or milk
½ cup brown sugar
1 tsp Brach's red hots (cinnamon) candy
1 Tbsp butter
½ cup white sugar
flour

Putting It Together

Chocolate Sauce
Heat but do not boil cream, butter, and candy in a saucepan. Stir until candy and butter is melted. Stir in chocolate until it is melted. Stir in brown and white sugar and cook over low to medium heat until sugar is dissolved. Slowly stir in flour until the mixture reaches a gravy-like thickness.

Turn heat down to low simmer, stirring occasionally.

Apples
Core apples and place in individual tin foil pockets. Add 1 Tbsp water to the bottom of each pocket and close tin foil tightly over apple.

Bake at 350° then remove from oven and serve hot with chocolate sauce.

Chickadee at Home

17

Osprey Fledglings

Great Horned Owlet

The Elk of Moraine Park

An Honest Man

During our first year on the ranch my father convinced the boss to let hunters onto the ranch as long as they obeyed some simple rules. These rules were posted on our lower gate where everyone had to see them as they entered the property.

"Please come to the house to ask permission and no shooting on the meadows."

Len came hunting every year, going to the same spot with the same results – nothing – but he always said he had a good time. About the fifth year Len came in and went to his spot. He came back to the house about 10:00 am just in time to see the owner of the ranch hanging a nice five-point bull elk up on the meat pole.

"Man! That's a nice elk. I seen one just like that this morning on the lower meadow," said Len. The owner allowed as that was where he shot this elk and asked why Len had not shot him.

Len answered, "The sign says no shooting on the meadows."

The rancher exclaimed "You can hunt any damn place on this ranch you want to!"

Later that day Len shot his first deer, a very nice buck. Yep, back down where he always hunted.

The Challenge

Night Flight

Fiery Sunset

Snow and Fire

24

Sauces

Storm Brewing

Sourdough Starter

The sourdough starter begins the fermentation process that is the foundation of any sourdough recipe. This can be prepared beforehand or can be prepared in camp if time allows. One note of caution whenever working with sourdough (starter, batter, or biscuits): do not use a metal bowl or utensils. This kills the starter.

What You Need

5 cups flour
2 tsp salt
2 Tbsp sugar
4 cups warm potato water

Putting It Together

Mix ingredients in a large bowl. Cover and let sit in a warm environment for 48 hours.

Sourdough Batter

The sourdough batter uses a portion of the sourdough starter to make bread or biscuits, leaving the rest of the starter to continue to age.

What You Need

1 cup starter
2 cups warm water
2½ cups flour
1 Tbsp sugar

Putting It Together

Loosely cover and let the batter sit a minimum of 6 hours or overnight.

Sausage Gravy

Increase or decrease amounts depending on number of servings.

What You Need

2 lbs. pork sausage
1 lb. Italian sausage
½ onion, chopped
flour
milk
salt, pepper, other seasoning to taste

Putting It Together

Fry meat, onions, and seasonings until done. Don't drain. Stir in flour until mixture is sticky. Stir in milk until gravy reaches desired thickness. Let mixture simmer on low heat for an additional 5-10 minutes, stirring frequently.

Enchilada Sauce

What You Need

1 large can tomato sauce (14.5 oz)
1 extra-large can tomatoes, diced (28 oz)
½ cup brown sugar
1 poblano pepper, chopped
3 tsp garlic, minced
1 Tbsp molasses
¼ tsp sage
1 onion, chopped

Putting It Together

Mix ingredients together in a large saucepan. Boil 20 minutes on medium heat. Simmer 20 minutes on low heat. Cool.

Hey, It's Cold Out Here

Frozen Dinner

Pinecones and Frost

Quick Breads

Spring Storm Colorado Style

Sourdough Biscuits

Now you can use the sourdough to make something you can enjoy.

What You Need

1 ½ cups basic sourdough batter
¼ cup softened butter
1 ¼ cups flour
1 Tbsp sugar
½ tsp salt
1 tsp baking powder

Putting It Together

Mix dry ingredients together in large bowl. Add butter and sourdough batter and stir until ingredients are well mixed. Place dough on a floured surface and knead 8-10 times or until dough is smooth and not sticky. Roll dough out to desired thickness. Cut dough with lightly floured biscuit cutter and place tightly together on an ungreased baking sheet.

Bake at 425° for 10-12 minutes or until tops are golden brown.

Baking Powder Biscuits

A staple for any self-respecting camp.

What You Need

2 cups flour
1 Tbsp sugar
1 tsp salt
2 ½ tsp baking powder
⅔ cup shortening or butter
1 cup milk, buttermilk, or warm water

Putting It Together

Mix dry ingredients in large bowl. Cut shortening or butter into dry ingredients with a pastry cutter or fork until the mixture has the consistency of coarse corn meal or has a bit of a greasy feel. Add liquid and fold mixture, kneading it until it is not knobby or sticky.

Place on floured surface and flatten by hand to desired thickness. Cut dough with a lightly floured biscuit cutter and place tightly together on an ungreased baking sheet.

Bake at 425° for 10-12 minutes or until tops are golden brown.

Corn Bread

This is my version of a classic camp favorite.

What You Need

1 cup flour
1 cup corn meal
¼ cup sugar
2 tsp baking powder
½ tsp salt
½ tsp baking soda
1 Tbsp vegetable oil
1 egg
¾ cup water

Putting It Together

Mix dry ingredients in a bowl. Mix oil, egg, and water together. Combine with dry ingredients to get a stiff batter.

Bake at 350° in a greased pan 14-15 minutes or until a toothpick stuck in the middle of the pan comes out clean.

Jackrabbit Enters Stage Right

Heron in Repose

Autumn Gold

Fall

Mid-September and Fall is in full color! An eerie sound floats upon the brisk, clear, early morning air. Unseen, a bull elk bugles at the timber's edge. Gear bags are checked, orange vest is ready, and the rifle is shooting straight. Hunting season will be upon us soon.

Three or four days before, we will set up camp at our favorite spot then cut wood and settle into our cozy canvas home for the next ten days. Old stories will be retold, and new adventures will be brought forth by all the guys and gals we share our camp with every year.

We hope there will be meat on the table this winter but, if not, being with all our friends will be reward enough until next year.

Elk Alert

Wilderness FedEx

Josephine's Cabin

Cow Camp

It rained during the night, a soft sound on the cabin roof.
When the old cowboy woke the next morning,
He stood on the porch at the dawn, with coffee and a biscuit in his hand.
Elk, at the meadow's edge, faded into the timber.
There was a chipmunk at his feet.

A rainbow crossed the western sky, it's colors bright in the early light.
Green made him think of the grass and the forest.
Yellow was the big warm sun peeking over the hill.
Red, blue, indigo, and violet were the flowers along the open hillside.
Orange, sunsets only God could make.

The cowboy looked down and smiled, the chipmunk was eating biscuit crumbs.
His bay horse whinnied a morning greeting.
It was a good day on the mountain.

Breakfast Feast

Laramie River Valley

Baked Casseroles

Just Missed

Green Bean Casserole

This might bring back memories of family get-togethers. It was very popular in the 1950s and 1960s. Everyone seemed to have a variation of this casserole. Here is mine.

What You Need

1 pkg frozen green beans
1 can cream of mushroom soup
1 can cream of celery soup
½ can milk
1 tsp garlic salt (season to own taste)
1½ cups cheddar cheese, grated (add as much as preferred)
2 cups Ritz crackers, crumbled (add as much as preferred)

Putting It Together

Boil green beans until tender. Mix soups, milk, garlic salt, together in bottom of a 9x13 inch casserole dish. Drain green beans and layer on top of soup mixture.

Bake at 350° until soup mixture comes to the top of the beans. Sprinkle cheese and cracker crumbles on top and heat until cheese melts (1-2 minutes).

Mac & Cheese Bake

Another favorite from the past that seems to be making a come-back. This recipe is good served with corn bread or biscuits and a green salad or coleslaw.

What You Need

1 pkg macaroni
1-2 cans cheese soup
½ can milk
1 lb. hamburger
½ lb. Italian sausage
1 small onion
1 cup cheddar cheese, grated (enough to cover top of dish)
1 small pkg sliced mushrooms

Putting It Together

Fill pan with water, add ½ tsp salt and bring to boil. Add macaroni and boil until soft. Drain and rinse. Fry hamburger, sausage, mushrooms, onion together. Season with salt, pepper, garlic or other seasonings as desired.

Empty soup into baking pan or Dutch oven and add just enough milk to spread soup evenly over bottom of pan. Spread ½ macaroni over soup. Spread all of meat mixture over macaroni layer. Spread rest of macaroni over meat.

Bake at 350° until soup bubbles up through the top layer. Add grated cheese to make a top cover and bake until cheese is melted.

Veggie Bake

Quick and easy baked dish. I usually use mixed vegetables, but any vegetable will work.

What You Need

1 large pkg any frozen vegetables
1 can cream of mushroom soup
2 eggs
1 cup Swiss cheese, grated
½ - ¾ soup can milk
1 tsp garlic salt (add as much as preferred)
½ tsp pepper (add as much as preferred)
2 cups Ritz or butter crackers, crumbled (add as much as preferred)

Putting It Together

Boil vegetables until almost done, drain. Mix soup and eggs and season to taste. Pour mixture into 9x13 inch baking pan and add vegetables. Sprinkle cheese over top to completely cover.

Bake at 350° for 20-25 min then cover with crumbled crackers.

Meat and Vegetable Pot Pie

I usually use ready-made pie crusts but if you are ambitious, you can try Melissa's pie crust recipe found in this book.

What You Need

2 lbs. ground beef, ground elk or, chicken
1 lg pkg any frozen vegetables
1 can cream of mushroom soup
2 eggs
1 cup cheddar cheese, grated
1 9-inch pie shell, double crust

Putting It Together

Boil vegetables until almost done, drain. If using chicken, boil until thoroughly cooked. If using ground beef or elk, fry until almost done. Mix soup and eggs and season to taste. Add meat and vegetables to soup mixture.

Pour mixture into bottom pie crust. Sprinkle cheese on top of pie filling and cover with top crust.

Bake at 400° for 30 minutes or until top crust is golden brown.

Avocet Delight

Chiles Rellenos José

This recipe is a favorite with my wife's family. It can be modified with spicier chiles and pepper seasoning to satisfy more "fiery" appetites.

What You Need

1 large can whole green chiles (~ 16 oz)
16 oz Monterey jack cheese
8 oz cheddar cheese, grated
5 large eggs
¼ cup flour
1 ¼ cups milk
½ tsp salt
Black pepper and liquid pepper to taste

Putting It Together

Cut Monterey jack cheese into 1 x 3 x ¼ inch slices. Rinse seeds from chiles, being careful not to tear the chile. Spread the chiles in a single layer on paper towels and carefully dry with another paper towel. Slip a slice of Monterey jack cheese into each chile.

Beat eggs and gradually add flour. Mix until smooth. Stir in milk, salt, and pepper.

Grease a 7x13 inch baking dish and arrange ½ of the chiles in the bottom. Sprinkle with the grated cheddar cheese. Repeat with another layer. Pour egg mixture over both layers.

Bake uncovered at 350° for 45 minutes or until firm. A toothpick inserted into the middle should come out clean.

Marty's Meat Muffins

This is a variation of Betty Crocker's Spanish meat loaf recipe. Marty hit on the idea of making individual servings in a muffin tin one day when she did not have enough time to cook a regular meat loaf. Using the muffin tin cuts down baking time by 15-20 minutes. One of our favorite variations is to mix ground beef and ground elk.

What You Need   makes 6 large or 12 regular muffins

1 ½ lbs. ground beef (or 12 oz ground beef and 12 oz ground elk)
8 oz tomato sauce
⅓ cup old-fashioned oats
1 egg
1 tsp salt
½ cup diced onions or mushrooms (optional)
garlic powder, pepper to taste

Putting It Together

Mix ground beef with ⅔ of tomato sauce. Add in remaining ingredients.

Grease a 6-12 count muffin tin, depending on serving size wanted. Use an ice cream scoop or large spoon to scoop meat mixture into each cup. Do not over fill. Spread remaining tomato sauce over top of each muffin.

Bake at 350° for 30-45 minutes or until cooked completely through.

Lasagna

Here is another of my wife's favorite recipes. It became a wedding rehearsal dinner tradition in her family. The original recipe called for 1 package dried Lowry spaghetti seasoning and an 8 oz. can of tomato sauce. In recent years it has been harder to find dry spaghetti seasoning, so my wife now substitutes a seasoned pasta sauce such as Ragu for the dried seasoning and the tomato sauce.

You can make up a batch and freeze it at home, then bake it in camp if that works better for you. Or you can just make it for dinner at home. That works also.

What You Need

1 lb. ground beef
3 ½ cups canned tomatoes, drained
8 oz seasoned pasta sauce
1 clove garlic, minced
8 oz no-boil lasagna noodles
16 oz cottage cheese, small curd
6-8 oz mozzarella cheese, cut into thin slices (⅛ to ¼ inch)
½ cup parmesan cheese, grated

Putting It Together

Brown meat and remove fat. Add pasta sauce and garlic. Cook for 40 minutes, stirring occasionally.

Grease a 9x13 inch pan and use one half of the ingredients to make a layer consisting of
Lasagna noodles, overlapping each by ½ inch
Meat mixture
Mozzarella cheese slices
Cottage cheese
Parmesan cheese
Add a second layer using remaining ingredients.

Bake at 350° for 30 minutes or until parmesan cheese is melted and a golden brown.

Morning Fog

Checking Out the Newbie

Bull Run

A nice fall afternoon turned into a two-day adventure when a friend and I started home from target shooting. We saw a Black Angus bull in the woods at the side of the road. We thought "Down here? There's no cattle down here." So we asked around and found out the bull was from a ranch eight miles to the north. We told the owner that "we will get him for you" when the owner assured us that the bull was gentle and halter broke.

The next morning three of us headed out on horseback for a meeting with Mr. Bull. As the only roper, I was to catch and hold the bull so he could be loaded into a horse trailer and taken home. We found the bull and herded him across the road to where the horse trailer was parked nearby. Now all I had to do was rope him and put him into the trailer. I stepped off my horse and cinched my saddle tighter. My first loop missed (I'm not a good heeler). My second loop caught one hind leg and I dallied off to my saddle horn, but by this time the bull was moving at a fast trot and going off a steep hill. My saddle slipped up my horse's neck almost to his ears when I tried to stop the bull. The result of a 950-pound horse against a 1,500-pound bull. Do the math.

Down the hill we went. The bull went one way around three small, dead aspens and I went the other. We stopped long enough to jerk my saddle back into place and pull the trees over on top of us. Then the bull headed down the hill once more, my horse and me following, until he went one way around a larger pine tree, I went the other, and everything came to a halt. Time to catch our breath because what went down that hill had to go back up that hill.

While we rested, one rider went back to the trailer to get a horse halter. The bull was halter broke, right? Wrong!! We got the halter on the bull and started to pull him back up the hill. After four or five steps he laid down. We let him rest then slapped him on the nose to get him up and headed up the hill only to do it all over again and again… until we reached the road and the horse trailer the owner had brought down. It was a 2-horse enclosed trailer — for a bull?? How were we going to get the bull loaded?

We maneuvered the bull to the back of the trailer, so he was looking into it. One person was up front at the escape door, ready to dive out. He waved at the bull who, still mad, charged into the trailer. Both doors were quickly slammed shut and the bull was captured.

The bull went back home and everyone else went out for burgers, pie, coffee, and retelling the events of the day.

Winter at Sprague Lake

Paintbrush and Pine

"Bobcat" Stew

No, I don't use bobcat meat, but as a kid I knew a man who, when he killed a bobcat, did make bobcat stew. His wife made him cook it out in the garage.

Good eat'n? He said so. I'll just take his word for it.

What You Need   makes 2-3 meals

    16 oz canned tomato sauce
    2 lbs. stew meat
    1-2 lg red potatoes (or 2 pkgs baby potatoes)
    1 small pkg baby carrots
    2 turnips
    2 rutabagas
    1 small onion
    3-5 stalks celery

Putting It Together

Chop onion and celery (use some of the celery leaves). Peel potatoes, turnips and rutabagas and cut into bite-sized chunks into large pot. Add carrots, meat and tomato sauce. Add enough water to cover everything. Season to taste (salt, pepper, garlic, etc.).

Bring to boil and boil for 10 minutes. Drop heat until water is just bubbling. Cover and let cook until all vegetables are cooked. Turn down heat to simmer until ready to serve, stirring occasionally.

Frying Pan Goulash

This is a quick and easy meal for those tough camping\hunting days when no one feels like cooking.

What You Need   serves 3-4

1 lb. hamburger
1 pkg mixed vegetables
1 small can tomato sauce (8 oz)
½ cup ketchup
¼ cup yellow mustard
2 Tbsp Worcestershire sauce
½ onion, chopped
salt, pepper, garlic, chili pepper, other seasonings to taste

Putting It Together

In large frying pan, fry hamburger until almost done. Add all other ingredients, cover, and cook over medium heat stirring occasionally. When the vegetables are cooked, it is ready to serve. Serve over biscuits, rice, or pasta.

What do I do now?

Fried Tacos

You can use tortillas or fry bread with this recipe.

What You Need

2 lbs. hamburger
1 lb. Italian sausage
1 can Bush's black beans (15-16 oz)
1 can chili beans (15-16 oz)
1 onion, chopped
1 chile pepper (your choice of heat)
1 pkg medium size flour tortillas
salt, pepper, or other seasoning to taste

Putting It Together

Mix all ingredients in a large frying pan and fry until done. Place taco mixture in a tortilla or fry bread and fold in half. Hold everything together with toothpicks.

Fill large saucepan or small stock pot half full of cooking oil and heat to boiling. Place taco in hot oil until golden brown.

March of the Trumpeter Swans

Linda's Calico Beans

This recipe comes from a member of my Square Dance exhibition team. Besides great dancers, there were also some excellent cooks.

What You Need

1 can green beans
1 can butter or yellow beans
1 can kidney beans
1 can baked beans
½ lb. bacon
½ lb. hamburger
¾ cup brown sugar
½ cup ketchup (or 1 small can tomato sauce)
1 small onion (diced)
2 tsp vinegar

Putting It Together

Fry bacon and hamburger, drain fat. Drain all beans except baked beans. Mix all ingredients in a casserole dish.

Bake at 350° for 40 minutes.

Winter Hawk

As the Clouds Part

White-breasted Nuthatch

Watching and Waiting

Yellow-bellied Marmot

Rolph the Viking (aka Vicky)

The first dog I remember having was a Norwegian Elk Hound we called Vicky. He was our family dog, calf finder, and meat saver. He also had a coyote girlfriend.

Our cattle ran on a meadow in the Spring that had 1½ miles of timber on both sides. During Spring calving season, we sometimes had a hard time finding the calves. If we saw a cow on the feed ground that had just had a calf we would take Vicky out and say "find the calf"! Vicky would take off into the timber and the cow, thinking her calf was in danger, would also take off, leading us right to her calf.

We never lost a game animal with Vicky along. If we wounded an elk or deer and it took off, Vicky was right on its trail. I never knew how he could pick the right trail out of the herd. Vicky was silent on the trail but at the end he had our game.

It was funny to see Vicky go after a marmot. First, if the marmot was too close to his den, Vicky would grab it by the rear, put on the brakes, and run backward until he had dragged the marmot to a safe distance away from the den. All the marmots I remember would sit up on their hind legs, ready to fight. This is just what Vicky wanted because he would circle the marmot at a trot. The marmot would pivot, keeping his face toward Vicky. Well, all that spinning got the marmot so dizzy that he couldn't stand up. Vicky watched for just that and bang he had a marmot by the back of the neck.

One night we came home about midnight and heard a ruckus in the barn. Out we all went to see Vicky and a badger laying down facing each other, so exhausted they couldn't get up. They had been after each other for a long time but neither dog nor badger had a scratch on them.

Once my mother shot a bobcat out of a tree and Vicky, thinking it was dead, jumped in to claim victory. The bobcat proved that it was not dead by scratching Vicky's nose. Vicky was furious so he resorted to the old "circle the marmot trick." It worked, and the bobcat ended his life a little dizzy.

Blue Columbine

Budding Alfalfa

Ghost Image

Water Lily Reflection

KeSa Mares

Horses and Camping — some simple advice

Camping with horses can be a fun way to explore the forests and wild areas of our country. But it also requires careful planning and extra care to ensure that both you and your horse have a good experience. Here are a few basic rules I have learned from growing up on a ranch and both camping and hunting with horses.

- If you are planning to pack in hay bales make sure you check with the agency that oversees your camping area (USDA, NPS, BLM, etc.). Most of these agencies require that you haul in certified weed free hay. An alternative is to feed dry pellets or cubed hay.

- Horses drink a lot of water! Especially when being fed dry pellets and cubed hay only. To avoid colic, make sure your horses have ready access to ample water.

- Horses need to lie down some, and roll.

- In Winter don't rub the snow off your horse's back. The snow is insulation, keeping heat in and your horse warmer.

- Before going camping, train your horse on picket, hobbles, or electric fence. That way they won't spook at whatever you are going to use to contain them.

- Carry a horse first aid kit: needle and thread, antiseptic ointment, bandages, grease for rope burns.

- Take basic shoeing equipment: hammer, rasp, nails.

- Take extra halters, bridles, and reins – they do get broken.

Fly Spray for all around use — Makes 1 quart

1 cup water
1 cup original *Avon Skin So Soft* Bath Oil
2 cups white distilled vinegar
2 Tbsp Eucalyptus Oil (found in health food stores)

Extra strength version: Don't add Water

Monarch Glory

Rocky Mountain Parnassian

Rawah Pronghorn

Sneak Peek

Night Camp

Camp

My door is always open
A warm fire in the stove

Have a cup of coffee
You're welcome to a meal

Grab a chair and set a spell
We'll spin a yarn or two

Glad you stopped and set awhile
Be careful and see you next year

Adiós my friend

The End

About the Authors

Dale Fry grew up on a ranch near Estes Park, Colorado. From a very young age he worked cattle with his father. A horse and a forest were his companion and playground. Both his parents taught him to cook and bake on a wood-fired kitchen stove. An early memory is of his first cherry pie that he made with home-canned cherries. He didn't realize until the pie was served that the cherries were unpitted. After high school, Dale spent three summers working for the US Forest Service in the Rawah Wilderness, and Laramie River Valley in northern Colorado and his love of that region was born. For the last forty years he has hunted and camped in this remote area. It was here that he experimented with camp cooking and with making the recipes his own.

Marty Fry grew up in Colorado and New Mexico. She spent weekends and vacations camping with her family and exploring the mountains near her home. Her favorite memories were of her father loading the family in a VW Bug and heading out into the hills to go "German Jeeping." She documented these trips with a Kodak Instamatic. She didn't pick up a SLR camera until after college when she worked as a historical archaeologist, photographing remains of historic mining camps in Ouray County, Colorado, and logging camps on the Mendocino Coast of California. Her love of photographing wildlife really took off when she discovered herons, egrets, northern shovelers, Canada geese, mallards, avocets, buffleheads, and other waterfowl crowding lakes in an open space near where she worked. Her images have won ribbons and awards in local county and state fairs and have appeared in several juried exhibits in Colorado. Her photographs of ranching life are on permanent display at the Colorado Department of Agriculture in Broomfield, Colorado.

www.ingramcontent.com/pod-product-compliance
Lightning Source LLC
Chambersburg PA
CBHW041105050426

42335CB00047B/159